THE BANANAS
B-GUIDE
TO SCHOOL
SURVIVAL

TO OUR PARENTS
who provided the first typewriter, and
when the earliest efforts were
unreadable, went right back out and
bought a new ribbon.

THE BANANAS B-GUIDE TO SCHOOL SURVIVAL

by
Pat & Joe Arthur

Illustrated by
Bob Taylor

SCHOLASTIC INC.
New York Toronto London Auckland Sydney

BANANAS Books are brought to you by BANANAS, today's most insane magazine for teenagers.

Editorial Director/BANANAS Books: Jane Stine.
Design Director: Bob Feldgus.
Production Editors: Sharon Graham and Juliet Seals-Leppert.

BANANAS Guide to Survival

ISBN 0-590-30028-8

12 11 10 9 8 7   8 9/8 01/9

Printed in the U.S.A.   01

Table of Contents

Official BANANAS School Readiness Test . 9

25 Mistakes I'm Not Going To Make
    Again This Year! 16

Who's Who in School 19

Becoming the BANANAS Student 28

Rumors that Have Been Going Around
    That You'll Want to Spread (But You'd
    Be A Fool To Believe) 38

Snap Courses 39

You Know It's Going To Be A Tough
    Class When 43

How To Translate Your Teachers 48

20 Things To Do In Study Hall — Not
    Including Studying 50

Coping With The Cafeteria 55

Subsisting With Substitutes 58

Locking In On Lockers 61

There's No Place Like Home — Ec. 64

Getting Into Trying Out 68

Quick Review Section 70

This Is A Test 77

The Last Word 94

Official Request-for-Pupil Form 95

Official Hall Pass Form 96

Introduction

OK, you're thumbing through *The BANANAS B- Guide To School Survival* and you're saying to yourself, "I've already got more school books than I'll ever learn how to read, so what makes these clowns think I need another one?" That's a good question. Another good question is, how long now have you been talking to yourself?

And while you're at it, you might as well try answering these:

- Would you recognize your locker blindfolded?
- What if the blindfold were on you and not the locker?
- You've got the confidence that comes from knowing you can tie your own shoes, but what if you were suddenly told you had to tie someone else's?
- You reported to the football field on the first day of practice, which is just fine; but isn't it also true when you asked the coach where he wanted to use you he said he already had a tackling dummy?
- You've passed a couple math courses and you can even change feet into metric units, but what about changing hands?

If your answer to any or all of these questions is, "Huh?" you probably need this book.

After all, no matter how far you go in life, one of the first places you're going to go is right through the schoolhouse door. Naturally you're worried about the pain of leaving, particularly if the door should be closed. And you want to leave because they've given you a diploma — not the boot.

But as you glumly look around from your back row corner desk, the one behind the big map of the Battle of Burgville in the War of the Polish Intermission, if it seems as if you've got a long climb ahead just to reach the bottom of the grading scale, this *BANANAS Guide* certainly won't hurt you. There's even an outside chance it might help.

For one thing, it will remind you that success in school is not necessarily the result of what you know, nor is it always a matter of who you know. Instead, success comes from knowing that you know what you think you know and who you know who knows it and knows you know it, know it or not. It also helps to know your own name. If you know all of this, and you'll know when you know it, there's no way to stop you from going on to know the type of person you have to be, the type who knows success is his and knows everyone else knows it, too.

Yes, *The BANANAS B- Guide to School Survival* can change your life, but remember, only *you* can change your socks!

Borrow a pencil or ask the attendant for a crayon and start taking your very own . . .

BANANAS School Readiness Test!

Instructions: You pick the right answers and let the ones that are left take care of themselves.

1. One statement *always* true of all statements on a True/False test is
   a) Short sentences are always true.
   b) Long sentences are always false.
   c) If a statement is partly true and partly false, the student should understand if he's not careful how he answers, he can be completely wrong — particularly if he is a she.
   d) Any sentence with a subjunctive involutional clause is true unless it is one of the 28,000 rare exceptions so peculiar to the English language, in which case it would be false.

2. You've noticed the even-numbered lockers are on the west side of the hall, while the odd-numbered lockers are on the east side. If your locker number is 329, you would find it
   a) by the smell.
   b) on the south side.
   c) a whole lot more pleasant if it weren't right next door to the new incinerator they use after lunch every day to burn the garbage.

3. The most important time to visit your counselor is
   a) when you want to find out who the tough, challenging teachers are so you can avoid them like the plague.
   b) when the hall duty teacher catches sight of you ducking out of the library on your way down to the lunchroom to see your boyfriend and you haven't got a pass.
   c) when you suddenly feel sick during the big science test you forgot all about.

4. The most important thing to remember about members of Student Council is that they
   a) decide such really important contemporary issues as whether the spring dance should be held in the lunchroom or the gymnasium.
   b) have been so skillful at scheduling their meetings during school hours that not one member has been present in a class where a quiz or test was being given in over two years.
   c) are actually robot spies for the vice-principal in charge of discipline.

5. Halfway through class the fire bell rings. You should
   a) put your head down on your desk again and try to get back to sleep.
   b) do just as the teacher orders — leave by the nearest exit even though the nearest exit is a window and you're on the third floor.
   c) ask for the hall pass so you can comb your hair before going outside where all your friends will see you.

d) crawl under your desk and cover your head.

e) recognize that crawling under your desk and covering your head is absurd and useless. Instead, cling to the teacher's skirt.

f) before it's too late go ahead and introduce yourself to the attractive new student you've been keeping an eye on for several months by saying: "Hey, listen, if you're not busy during the fire drill or anything would you like to burn up with me?"

6. Being sent to the office probably means

a) your little joke involving the swimming pool and the ton of lime jello didn't go over quite as well as you hoped.

b) the principal wants to tell you he's called your parents to tell them what a great job you're doing in all your classes, then he's going to buy you lunch.

c) you're the one millionth student to pass through the school's front door and they want to present you with your prize, a new Trans-Am.

7. It is the responsibility of the class president to

a) stand around smiling and being friendly even though he probably doesn't have the slightest idea who you are.

b) make campaign speeches promising to change things around school in ways the Board of Education wouldn't allow in a thousand years.

c) make sure the homecoming queen has dates every Friday and Saturday night — with him!

8. The registration room teacher hands you your new schedule and right away you notice eight of the nine periods are filled with study halls. This means
   a) you graduated a year ago and ought to be out looking for a job.
   b) the schedule they've given you will teach you as much about computer programming as the person knew who programmed the computer that made up your schedule.
   c) they're going to have to change your schedule if they seriously expect you to have enough time during the day to get all your homework done.

9. Schedules should be changed
   a) when they start to smell.
   b) before they start to smell.
   c) in private.
   d) only after you've talked it over with people who know what they're talking about — your friends.

10. The term "lunch line" means
    a) what a boy says to a girl while they're sitting in the cafeteria.
    b) a group of people standing in a row waiting to throw up.
    c) both D & E.

11. When a teacher turns on the lights in the classroom to change film reels, you should
    a) wake up.
    b) at least stop snoring.
    c) go out for popcorn.

ANSWER KEY: In the multiple choice section, item number B is the correct response about 15% of the time. Number D is the answer to the questions lettered 2, 3, 5, 7, 9, 10, 11, and 12. The odd-numbered questions are A, C, and F in reverse order alternately. All five of the true/false items are true except for numbers 17, 18, 19, and 20. The answer to the extra-credit item is "Donny Osmond."

WHAT YOUR GRADE MEANS:

If you scored—

350 thru 301... There must be some mistake. The highest grade possible is 300. Check back over your work. Did you remember to divide by pi? Then by cake?

300 thru 201 ... You are an exceptional student. Only two human beings have ever scored this high. One of them wrote the test and the other was caught copying from him.

200 thru 101 ... If your grade has been figured correctly, you can probably get through life without reading *The BANANAS B-Guide To School Survival.* On the other hand, anyone with your intelligence has to be a real nerd to spend valuable time taking this stupid test, therefore the book is for you.

100 thru 51 ... Fully one-half of the students who took this Official

BANANAS School Readiness Test while it was still being perfected and standardized scored in this range. The other student never showed up.

50 thru 4 . . . Anyone who scores in this range has got to be kidding. Either that, or you copied your answers off a hamster. You are *exactly* the kind of person who will benefit most from *The BANANAS B-Guide To School Survival*. Simply leaf through the book and in no time at all, perhaps less, you'll have figured out which way's up, which side of the book opens, and which side you're on!

When you think you're ready, take the BANANAS School Readiness Test over again. Statistics show each time a student retakes the BSR Test, he raises his grade an average of 5 points. At that rate you'll pass it easily—after only 39 more tries!

So you didn't score too well on the BANANAS School Readiness Test and you say last school year wasn't your finest hour? Don't worry—this year is going to be different. Now, thanks to *The BANANAS B- Guide,* you're not going to make the same mistakes this year—you're going to make new ones! One student has made the mistake of making a list of the mistakes he's not going to make again this year. You're not going to make the mistake of reading it, are you?

25 Mistakes I'm Not Going To Make Again This Year!

1. This year when they tell us to dress for gym, I'm not going to put on a tuxedo.

2. Since I flunked Math IV last year, I'm not going near that class this year. This year I'm taking Math V.

3. If I can help it, I'm not going to the homecoming dance again with my sister.

4. Not only am I going to memorize the combination to my locker, I'm going to remember which floor it's on.

5. I don't care how good the other students say it is, when I go to the cafeteria I'm not going to order my liver cooked rare.

6. When a teacher asks me a question in class, I'm not going to say, "Who wants to know?"

7. I'm going to try to take part in after-school activities other than detention.

8. I've got to start watching my weight, so I'm not going to fill up on junk food between meals every day. I'm going to have it all at once in place of breakfast.

9. This year I'm not going to work after school unless I can find a job.

10. I'm not going to ask for dates by saying to the girl, "I'm sure you've got better things to do, but. . ."

11. I'm not going to wait until May to wash my gym clothes.

12. I'm not giving my friends any more rides to school unless they get on my back in such a way that I don't have to stoop down.

13. This year I'm going to wear matching shoes.

14. There's no rule that says you have to eat in the same part of the cafeteria the whole time you're in school, so this year I'm going to eat in the section with tables and chairs.

15. I'm going to start an exercise program. Every day I'm going to do at least five sit-downs.

16. Last year I took an inch. This year I'm taking a mile.

17. Last year, someone would borrow a pencil from me just about every day and I'd never see it again. Well, they're not getting any more pencils. This year I'm carrying pens.

18. Last year, the teachers brought the textbooks out of the bookroom in September, handed them out to us to hold until June, when they collected them again and carried them back to the bookroom. Our teachers are too overworked already. I'm going to ask them to leave out the first two steps.

19. Since I'm not old enough to have a driver's license, it was embarrassing last year when my mother drove me on dates. I've had enough of that. This year I'm going to ask my father to drive.

20. My parents say I take too many Mickey Mouse courses. No more of that. I've signed up for 20 credits in my major subject—cartooning.

21. Last year, when someone in class hit the kid next to him or threw a paper airplane, I told the teacher who did it. That was wrong. This year I'm going to wait for the teacher to ask.

22. If a teacher says you can sit wherever you want, no more first row for me. I'm going to sit out in the parking lot.

23. The folks are always after me to go out for sports. So I think I might join that group that practices throwing dice every afternoon out behind the stadium.

24. A lot of my friends buy bubblegum cards as I do. It's a great hobby. But this year, to make it more interesting, I'm going to collect the cards instead of the gum.

25. I was tardy too often last year. This year, I'm going to correct that. If it looks like I'm going to be late, I'm taking the whole day off!

Face it, it's a jungle out there. And wearing a pith helmet and safari shorts isn't going to get you very far! (It might get you to the nurse's room for a short rest, however!) What you've got to do is take a good look at the competition— your fellow students. No—put down the binoculars. All you need is this handy guide to. . .

Who's Who In School

TYPE #1: The All-American Boy

This poor soul, condemned to life with Robert Redford looks, saddled with the popularity and prestige that go with being unanimously elected team captain, not to mention stuck dating the head cheerleader eight nights a week. He is usually six foot four and called names like Lance William Hollingsworth or Randall Stanford Baird. There are those who call him other names, but they, in turn, are called jealous.

APPEARANCE: This clothes horse trots out a parade of every brand name known to man and impressive to women. Plus he's got a low-numbered football jersey, and a formerly straight nose given lots of character by character-building athletics and the semi-skilled hands of a part-time plastic surgeon. The pom pom girls draped on each arm form human book ends for the only school book he ever carries, his playbook.

FAVORITE COLOR: The color they use to make the American flag.

FAVORITE TV SHOW: *Sesame Street*. (He can already count higher than a third of the Muppets.)

FAVORITE MUSIC: Dentist office music.

FAVORITE CLASS: Phys. ed.

LAST BOOK READ: Little Black Book.

FAVORITE SAYING: "I've got to leave class early again for football practice."

TYPE #2: The Girl You Wish Lived Next Door

Head cheerleader by divine right, she's followed her teams through a hundred big games and enthusiastically led the cheers of a thousand gawking fans. To do this she's had to focus her complete attention on practicing, exercising, and dieting since preschool, and when the season's over she's even going to read a couple of pamphlets on sports to find out what all the shouting's about.

APPEARANCE: What a wardrobe! Her designer jeans fit so snugly that she has to stand up to sit down! Everything she wears has the label on the outside, which is just as well, since that's her only reading material! Her hair is naturally curly, and she spends hours each week at the beauty parlor making it naturally curly! Her closet must simply be brimming with clothes that are the products of hardworking silkworms, the finest British sheep, and whatever animal it is that gives nylon.

FAVORITE COLOR: Blonde.

FAVORITE TV SHOW: Miss America Pageant.

FAVORITE CLASS: Anything taught by a man.

FAVORITE SAYING: "I really wish I could be here to take that test, Mr. Snookums, but I've got to get back down to Florida to work on my tan."

FAVORITE MUSIC: Likes '50s Rock & Roll. While others have gone on to accept the newer Rock music, she prefers Roll music.

LAST BOOK READ: *Swooning In The Moonlight* by Barbara Cartland.

GOAL IN LIFE: To find an eye shadow that's really *her!*

TYPE #3: Punk

Not yet old enough to shave, he carries a blade nonetheless. And just as he wouldn't think of letting anyone push him around, neither would he think of letting anyone stop him from pushing them around. In fact, he wouldn't think if his life depended on it, which, the way things are going for him, it probably will. Known, feared, and avoided by almost everyone, his teachers call on him daily, either to find out if he's cutting again or to tell him to get out. There are those, however, who say he wouldn't hurt a fly, and for proof they point to the fly buzzing undisturbed around his scraggly head.

APPEARANCE: His rock group T-shirt bursts at the seams, especially where it's stretched thin over the chip on his shoulder. The sullen, cold blue eyes are complemented by the hot blue jeans. You know they're hot because the label's been filed down. He stands tall in his stack-heeled motorcycle boots, this proud possessor of unkempt straight hair down to where his belt would be if he hadn't used the leather to wrap his blackjack, and a curled lip where a smile would go if he weren't afraid he'd break his own face.

TATTOO ON ARM: "Born To Take Shop."

FAVORITE COLOR: Black and blue.

FAVORITE TV SHOW: "Curdled Blood Theatre" on Fridays at midnight.

FAVORITE MUSIC: Has every Punk Rock album ever made, a few of which he even paid for.

FAVORITE CLASS: Remedial metal shop.

LAST BOOK READ: *Sally And Spot Learn To Read*.

FAVORITE SAYING: "Say that again and see what happens!"

GOAL IN LIFE: Hang loose.

TYPE #4: A Fine Example

This one's called the Teacher's Pet because she dogs her teacher's footsteps or stays so close to his desk you're sure she's on a leash. When she's not clapping erasers, she's applauding lectures. Only 15 and already she's got chalkboard hands. The number of miles she's jogged running errands could qualify her for the Olympics. The teacher she does all these favors for has talked her into becoming a teacher herself because he told her there's always some kid around who'll get a big thrill out of doing all the dirty work.

APPEARANCE: Trying to be the perfect young lady, she acts and dresses like a little old lady. Sometimes she lets go and wears her T-shirt that says "Geometry isn't just for squares." She has the clean, well-scrubbed smell that comes from bathing in Lysol.

FAVORITE COLOR: Institutional beige.

FAVORITE TV SHOW: When no one can see her she locks the door and turns on *The Gong Show*.

FAVORITE MUSIC: Chants.

FAVORITE CLASS: All of them!

LAST BOOK READ: *The Fall of the Roman Empire* (just for fun!)

FAVORITE SAYING: "I'm not wasting any of my valuable study time out on a date with some silly boy, even if one ever asks me."

GOAL IN LIFE: To be a teacher just like Mr. Dipson, bringing enlightenment and pencils to those who have neither.

Becoming the
BANANAS Student

Now that you've got some idea who's who and who you don't want to be, why not give some thought to becoming the resourceful, clever type who doesn't need to rely on above-average intelligence, good looks, and athletic ability to get the high grades and impressive letters of recommendation others take for granted. And while you're thinking it over, ask yourself this question: Do you really have any choice? Then set about becoming. . .

TYPE #5: The BANANAS Student

Remember, if you look like a good student, you are a good student. The right clothes and props are essential. Keep in mind that it's traditional for brainy kids to pay very little attention to clothes. If you must dress in style, at least make sure that your clothes do not fit. Wear glasses whether you need them or not. Don't comb your hair. Wear lace-up Hush Puppies (keep them untied) or galoshes. Wear a size 48 belt. For some reason, smart students always seem to have a lot of extra belt hanging down.

Always carry a pencil behind your ear and keep a row of pens clipped to your shirt pocket. Place inkstains on several fingers each morning to show that you are serious enough to use a fountain pen. For extra credit, you will want to appear to have a slide rule and a calculator attached to your belt. But don't go to the expense of buying these costly items you will

never use. Simply buy the carrying cases and attach them to your belt.

Carry all of your textbooks with you to all of your classes. Wrinkle and smudge the covers so they will appear to have been carried home often. At the beginning of each school year, go through all your textbooks and underline every other paragraph. This is a time-consuming job, but it need only be done once. When your teacher has seen what a thorough underlining job you are doing, you need never open the book again.

Act Like a Student, Look Like a Student

Some General Rules

1. Look the teacher in the eye when he or she is talking. Occasionally nod yes — no matter what he or she is saying. From time to time, say aloud, "How true, how true."
2. Always say as little as possible. The more you talk, the sooner they'll realize that you don't know what day it is. Whenever another student gives a wrong answer, laugh loudly to show that you would never make such a foolish mistake.
3. When you are called on, never admit that you haven't heard the question. Instead, say: "I'm sorry. I was thinking about Man's place in the ecosystem." Or try: "I was writing down your last point so that I can do further research on it tonight at the library instead of going home to dinner."

4. When taking a test, always raise your hand and say, "Miss Fosdick, could you give me an extra sheet of paper to use to cover my answers?"

5. Never leave a class without going up and saying something impressive to your teacher. Say: "I watched the most wonderful show on the educational channel last night." Leave before he can find out that you're talking about *Monty Python*.

6. If these tips do not help, you may want to try something extreme for extra credit. Try a large tattoo on your writing arm. For best results, it should be a big red heart with the word "Teacher" emblazoned across it.

Questions To Distract and Impress

A good question asked at the beginning of class can sidetrack the class completely and get you out of the day's lesson that you know nothing about. Here are some good questions that are guaranteed to be time-consuming.

1. If it's true that the earth is tilted on its axis, how come we don't have to shorten the legs on one side of our tables?

2. In prison breaks, convicts always escape by carving guns out of soap. Why don't they ever carve knives?

3. Is capital punishment severe enough?

4. Does the DC-10 eat its young?

5. Someone on TV said that if you stay home on Election Day it's the same as a vote for the winner. Since I always like to vote for a winner, doesn't it make sense for me to stay home?

6. If it's true that a dog is man's best friend, why don't people ever want to be seen at a dance with one?

Talk Smart, Be Smart

From time to time, your teacher might ask you a question that could lead to embarrassment or downright disgrace. Be prepared for these instances. Snappy answers to difficult questions should be rehearsed until they come naturally to you. Here are a few examples to practice on:

Teacher: George, you don't have your book open. Turn to page 53!
BANANAS Student: What page would that be in the metric system?

Teacher: Marvin, didn't I see you out in the parking lot this period yesterday with Mary Sue Bond?
BANANAS Student: Could you describe her?

Teacher: Sarah, take the chalk from my desk and put problem number six on the board.
BANANAS Student: Cough! Cough! I will, but first could you tell us again the symptoms of white lung? Cough! Cough!

Teacher: Harry, why don't you share what you were whispering with the entire class?
BANANAS Student: I would, but I've heard that compliments make you blush.

Teacher: Marge, your history notebook's filled with blank pages.
BANANAS Student: I know. You're always so rushed on notebook-checking day I just thought I'd lighten your burden.

Teacher: What can you tell me about the Civil War?
BANANAS Student: Only that the way we live would be vastly different if the Civilians had won.

Teacher: Lester, would you like to be the person in class who collects papers?
BANANAS Student: Could you get someone else? I already collect stamps.

Surefire Excuses

Situation One: Excuses For When You're Late To Class

It's the weirdest thing! During the night, some prowlers broke into our house. They didn't take anything, but they set back all our clocks 20 minutes!

No, I'm not late for *today's* classes. I'm the first one here for *tomorrow's!*

I can't help it. Ever since my aunt bought me a metric clock, I don't know *what* time it is!

My alarm clock did go off — off with another alarm clock!

Situation Two: Excuses For When You Didn't Do The Homework Assignment

I'm really sorry. When you said it was due the 31st, I thought you meant February!

I did the assignment, but when I got to school, all the pages were blank. I think someone slipped me some invisible ink!

Why don't I just wait till after graduation? Then when I'm settled, I'll mail it to you.

I haven't got the homework, but how about a joke instead? What's green and red and goes 90 miles an hour?

Situation Three: General Purpose Classroom Excuses

Even if this trick knee I've got doesn't act up on the way to the blackboard, I'd never be able to write anything up there because of my trick wrist.

The reason I don't have my textbook is it's being held by a third party as my bet. I bet Kelvin Osgood that you'd win any poll taken to find out who the friendliest, most understanding teacher in the building is.

All I can say is I don't have my committee report ready today for the same reason I didn't have that book report back in January — my Uncle Fred in Cleveland passed away again.

It isn't that I object to sitting in the front row, it's just that my optician said I should be as close to natural lighting as possible and the way the sunshine's reflecting off that girl's red hair back there by the window, I just thought the seat next to her would be a much better place for me to sit, medically speaking, of course.

Situation Four: Excuse Notes To Bring From Home

Please excuse my daughter Rosie from homework, research papers, book reports, quizzes, tests, and examinations because she is allergic to notebook paper. Our doctor assures us, however, that she may take part in all other classroom activities.

Please excuse Ruth from school all this week, next week, and the week after, as she's got an appointment to have her teeth cleaned.

Please excuse Marvin's tardiness this morning. His bicycle wouldn't start.

Red Rover, Red Rover, send Ralph right over.

Please dismiss Rodney from school 15 minutes early today as he's got a plane to catch and he needs time to get on his running shoes.

Rumors That Have Been Going Around That You'll Want To Spread (But You'd Be a Fool To Believe)

1. Sour old Miss Finch, the school's librarian since 1930, was once a famous movie star.

2. The Department of Health, Education, and Welfare is going to require that all difficult tests carry a mental health warning.

3. Some court in Washington just ruled that whenever a teacher calls on a student to recite in class, the teacher must inform the student of his right to remain silent and that anything he says may be used against him in a grade book.

4. An independent research lab discovered it's the ink used in mimeograph machines to print tests, worksheets, and reading lists that causes pimples.

5. In addition to the three snow days the schools already have, the Board of Education's allowing three days off for sunshine.

The **BANANAS** student knows it takes more than hard work to graduate. It takes around 17 credits. The typical student gets these by fighting his way through Renaissance Authors or being embarrassed every time the physics teacher hands back a test, but our **BANANAS** student rises to the challenge by ducking the drudgery. Instead of studying a civics textbook, the **BANANAS** student reads a course description pamphlet, then fills his schedule with ...

SNAP COURSES!

#103 INTRODUCTION TO PREPARING BETWEEN MEAL SNACKS. 5 periods mid-morning, 5 periods afternoon. 1 credit, 9,575 calories. Instructor: Mr. Pringle.

Teaches the student simple recipes calling for Doritos, Cheez-its, and a bowl.

#127 CRUISING. 10 periods, 2 credits. Instructors: Mr. Kuralt, Ms. Guthrie.

Enrollment is limited to the first 25 students with gasoline charge cards. Those taking this course gain actual on-the-road as well as drive-in experience. A full 10 minutes of classroom work each week is required with special units including: Shortcuts Using Little Traveled Dead End Streets; It Might Be His Car But How Often Should Dad Be Allowed To Drive It? and Self-Serving Without Guilt.

#141 USE & MAINTENANCE OF THE #2 PENCIL. 3 periods, 1 credit. Instructors: Mr. Eberhard, Ms. Faber.

Units include: The Pencil As A Fashion Accessory: Behind Which Ear? and Tips On Sharpening Wooden and Mechanical Pencils. For those students who regularly chew their pencils, a special lab project provides the opportunity for taste-testing the major brands such as Reliance, Venus Velvet, and Your Name Here. Classroom activities include lectures, committees, film-strips, and a term paper that must be written in ink.

#153 A SURVEY OF TODAY'S MUSIC. 5
periods, 1 credit, 75 decibels. Instructor:
Mr. Kasem.

Mellow rock, country rock, punk rock, hard
rock, moon rock — all the world's important
music is heard in this comprehensive course.
Using miniature receivers from Hong Kong and
lightweight single earphones, the students
quickly come to recognize highly significant
popular music trends from A to Z, number 1 to
number 40.

#221 FAST FOODS AS YOUR DIET. 5
periods, 1 credit, 0.3 grams protein, 98
grams carbohydrate. Instructors: R.
McDonald, B. King, P. Hut.

Teaches the student how to remove his supper
from a paper bag.

**#275 CONTEMPORARY LIFE AS SEEN
ON TV.** 7 periods, 3 credits, 12 channels.
Instructors: Mrs. Kotter, Mr. Carson.

The perfect course for students who have been
getting too much exercise. By electing this
course they commit themselves to viewing a
minimum of six hours of TV every day. They are
further required to watch a color set, uninter-
rupted by household chores or homework, and to
be assured of qualifying for the full three credits, students must perform at least 85% of their
viewing while lying down. Special topics include: Valuable Lessons We Can Learn From
Commercials About Life; Death And Shopping;
The TV Guide As Literature; and Cable TV In
Your Car.

#289 **NOTEBOOKKEEPING.** 2 periods, .5 credits. Instructor: Mr. Cratchet.

The student will master the skill of aligning holes in filler paper with notebook rings. Special mini-unit on illustrating the inside covers with drawings of Cupid shooting one arrow into a heart with initials, another in the direction of a favorite date, and the third, fourth, and fifth in the direction of the vice-president in charge of discipline.

#324 **WALT DISNEY'S AMERICA.** 4 periods, 1 credit, 3 "E" Coupons. Instructor: Ms. Poppins.

This is the Mickey Mouse course every student's heard so much about. Movies, comics, picture books, and lithographed lunch boxes concentrate on Mickey's life, beginning with his difficult birth at which Walt Disney lost four pints of ink and for a while they thought they might have to call for an eraser. The course continues through the Hollywood years to the near fatal accident following his 50th birthday party when a mousetrap under the speakers' table malfunctioned, throwing Mickey across the room where he narrowly missed landing in a paper shredder.

Let's face it, not every course will be a snap — even the BANANAS student will come up against the kind of class that's so tough the only time anybody got an A was when the computer made a mistake. How can you tell if you're in for one of these killer classes? Well, here are some tips from the *BANANAS B-Guide* on what to look out for.

You Know It's Going To Be A Tough Class When. . .

You know it's going to be a tough class when some of the students leaving the room are crying so hysterically it's obvious they'll have to stop by the restroom to pull themselves together before going on to football practice.

You know it's going to be a tough class when there are scratches on the glass in the classroom door that could have been made only by human fingernails.

You know it's going to be a tough class when you look around and there's no movie screen.

You know it's going to be a tough class when the winner of last year's Superior Student Award got a C—.

You know it's going to be a tough class when it's an elective course and only two of you have elected to be in the classroom, the other person being the teacher.

You know it's going to be a tough class when you walk into the room and there's no back row.

45

You know it's going to be a tough class when the teacher hands out a seven-pound textbook and says, "This is volume one."

You know it's going to be a tough class when it takes two entire evenings just to read the reading list.

You know it's going to be a tough class when the office helpers who bring notes up from the principal slip them under the door.

You know it's going to be a tough class when you look around the second day and see the entire chess team and no one from the football team.

You know it's going to be a tough class when you discover a message under your desk that reads: HELP! I'M TRAPPED IN THIS HORRIBLE CLASS AND I MAY NEVER SEE MY TELEVISION AGAIN!

Talk to your counselor, talk to your best friend, talk to yourself — they'll all tell you the same thing. A student can have 20/20 hearing, brand-new contact lenses in smart, designer frames, even a pencil with its own eraser, but to have a shot at the really super grades parents demand and fast food chains give away free cheeseburgers for, you have to study not only your Spanish and shorthand notes, but your teachers as well. While you're certainly doing the right thing translating textbook exercises, it's even more important that you learn. . .

How To Translate Your Teachers

"Our next unit is really going to challenge your thinking."
Translation: The next unit is really going to be hard.

"We should appreciate all the time and work our lunchroom staff puts into decorating the cafeteria and making it a bright, attractive place where we can eat our lunches."
Translation: The food's garbage.

"I'd hoped to have all the reports graded and back to you today, but an emergency came up last night, so there are still a few I haven't finished reading."
Translation: Teachers like Monday Night Football too, you know.

"We're having some technical problems, so the educational film I said we'd see today has to be canceled."

Translation: She forgot to order the movie.

"Since there's not more than 45 minutes left in the period and problem sixteen's got five separate steps, let's save it for tomorrow and skip on to number seventeen."

Translation: He left his answer key at home.

"We had a few more failing grades on this test than we usually have."

Translation: She put a dozen of her best trick questions on this one.

"When I was in school the teachers always seated us according to the alphabet. I didn't see anything wrong with it then and I don't see anything wrong with it now that I'm the teacher."

Translation: Before she got married her last name was Ziffel.

"You'll be having a substitute next week because I was fortunate enough to be elected delegate to the National Teachers' Association convention in Ft. Lauderdale. I'll be listening to speeches and attending all kinds of workshops that'll help me prepare better, more interesting lessons."

Translation: While the class is up here filling out worksheets, he'll be heading for the beach.

Any fool can report to study hall with a
book bag full of work to do, but it takes
the BANANAS student, a very special
fool, to figure out. . .

20 Things To Do In Study Hall — Not Including Studying

1. Begin digging an escape tunnel under your desk.

2. You can kill a little time writing your name in the textbooks you'd want returned if you lost them. This is a perfect activity for one of those days you don't have a pencil.

3. While the other students are making paper airplanes, you make a paper airport.

4. Be a clock watcher. See if you can figure out how long it takes the second hand to make one complete revolution. Now do the same thing with the first hand.

5. Index all the names carved in the top of your desk.

6. Turn the top of your desk into a chain letter.

7. Update the Little Black Book that is the cornerstone of your fantastic social life by alphabetizing both names.

8. Reach under the top of your desk and start a chewing gum collection.

9. Separate and catalog your gum collection on the basis of weight, color, bubble or regular, sugar or artificial sweetener, and whether a given wad appears to have been abandoned or merely parked until some future study hall.

10. Read a comic book and if the teacher says anything, tell him you're doing a report on American Pop Art.

11. Read a skateboarding magazine and if the teacher says anything, tell him you're doing a report on transportation.

12. Write a couple of notes.

13. Write a whole song.

14. If you just came from the school cafeteria, or you have to eat there next period, make out your Last Will & Testament just in case there are any problems with unpleasant side effects again this week.

15. When you ask for the hall pass, don't say which restroom you're going to, then go to the one next to the Haunted Mansion at Disney World.

16. Make a flip movie by drawing stick figures on the outside margins of your history book.

17. Your flip movie can be "Edited for Television" by cutting out two entire chapters and that page of difficult review questions on the stock market crash.

18. Now that the epic flip movie's finished, turn your thoughts to how you can raise enough money to pay the rather steep book-defacing fine you'll owe at 50¢ a page.

19. Press a rose between the pages of your old literature book. Rose is the girl in the third row who keeps pestering you to help her with her adverbs.

20. Tell the teacher you'd like to take some of the extra textbooks and papers you've been carrying around all day to your locker, so you wondered if you could use the Haul Pass.

Coping With The Cafeteria

In really fine restaurants (the ones with signs out front saying you've got to wear a shirt and shoes), customers often order their meals in French. Your school cafeteria is different. For one thing, it's not a fine restaurant. It's probably not even a fair restaurant. If you don't believe this, when was the last time you heard anyone ask for a doggie bag? What you have heard is, "I guess I'll have some of that green stuff there."

So you'll have a better idea of what you're ordering, the *BANANAS B- Guide* helpfully provides you with this. . .

OFFICIAL CAFETERIA COLOR EQUIVALENCY CHART

Color of Stuff	What It Might Be
brown	the tray for carrying stuff
	mud pie
	stewed prunes
	sober prunes
	charcoal broiled schoolburger
black	charcoal
reddish-purple	Harvard Beets
bluish-gray	High School Beets

Color of Stuff	What It Might Be
orange	orange juice
chartreuse	chartreuse juice
yellow (solid)	wax beans
	wax banana (ripe)
	powdered eggs
	carpet sample
	chunks of cheese remaining after traps are baited
yellow (liquid)	beaten powdered eggs
	day-old milk
	fresh government surplus chocolate milk
	well water
dark yellow (liquid)	not-so-well water
green	french fries — St. Patrick's Day
	soyburger (rare)
	soyburger (well done)
	12″ soy pizza
	wax banana (unripe)
green (large portion)	head of lettuce
green (small portion)	foot of lettuce
green (tossed, partially eaten)	chef's salad
moss green	green moss
red	fresh apple peels
white, red, and pink	cutsie decorations put up for Valentine's Day by one of the cooks

Color of Stuff	What It Might Be
yellowed white, faded red, and flecked pink	Valentine's Day decorations from 1974
white and institutional green	vanilla ice cream topped with paint flakes from the cafeteria walls
black and white	tapioca pudding with flies
multi-colored spots	plate from yesterday's lunch they forgot to stick in the dishwasher — usually half price!
reddish-orange	Jello mold
gray-green	bread mold
colorless (liquid)	empty 16 oz. Jumbo Size glass that goes with the Budget Lunch
	10 oz. glass of SchoolCola
colorless (solid)	"He-Man Cut" Roast Beef au Lucite
maple	drum stick
bleached white	wishbone
light brown, yellow, and white	peanut butter and mustard sandwich
blue	nerf cake
pale yellow (filled with small holes)	sponge cake
pale yellow (filled with large holes)	sponge

Subsisting With Substitutes

There will be days when as much as your regular teacher wants to be with you in school expanding your awareness by lecturing you into a deep sleep, it just isn't possible. Illness, family business, catching up on a favorite soap opera are two of the acceptable reasons teachers may use to request a substitute for their classes. Thus, from time to time and plot twist to plot twist, you will be faced with adjusting to the strange new ways of a strange new teacher.

Now, sad to say, there are some students for whom the sight of a substitute nervously writing his or her name on the blackboard is an instant invitation to pull unspeakable pranks (which they will talk about for weeks afterward). A few words of warning to these students. . .

A complete list of every prank, trick, and joke you can play on the substitute without getting into big trouble:

1.
2.
3.
4.
5.

The BANANAS student, of course, knows that pranking the substitute is just a waste of energy. (To the BANANAS student, staying

awake is a waste of energy.) As always, the
BANANAS student's mind is fixed on survival.
With this goal in mind, the BANANAS student
sails past substitutes with the famous creative
question and answer game — which the authors of this book have kindly included in this
chapter — here — right now....

Substitute's Question: What page did you
leave off with at the end of class yesterday?
Your Answer: Page 21 in the *TV Guide.* We
were trying to decide which game show to watch
in class today.

Substitute's Question: How long after the bell
rings does your teacher normally start marking
people tardy?
Your Answer: About 45 minutes.

Substitute's Question: According to the instructions your teacher left, he handed out worksheets to half the class yesterday and said the rest of you could share. Now could I see the hands of those of you who received the worksheets?

Your Answer: I think the reason nobody put his hand up is that the half of the class that got the worksheets, strange as it may seem, is absent.

Substitute's Question: I see by the sign-up sheet we've got a clown in here who signed his name "Jim Nasium." OK, which one of you is Jim Nasium?

Your Answer: Don't look at me! You're not gonna pin this one on old Bill Fold!

Substitute's Question: I've just been hit with a paper wad, and unless one of you can give me a good reason why that should happen in a classroom full of students your age, I'll feel perfectly justified in my opinion that there's simply no excuse for this kind of behavior.

Your Answer: Actually, we've been studying primitive man and how he probably calculated the trajectory of a hand-launched, heavier-than-air projectile because our regular teacher told us a strong America needs scientifically-minded students who are willing to experiment even at the risk of angering a few of our shortsighted citizens who happen to have some silly objection to being used as targets.

Locking In On Lockers

If school survival were only a matter of what happens in the classroom ... this would be a much shorter book. Luckily, the BANANAS student needs help not only in the classroom but in the halls as well. At least that's our excuse for including one entire chapter on lockers.

Locker Selection

- Choose an end locker so you'll have: (1) a better view, (2) more elbow room, (3) cross ventilation, and (4) a prime location in case a developer's looking around for a corner that still doesn't have a gas station.

- Be sure the locker you choose isn't on the east wall next to the patio, because that's the wall shown in the architect's drawing of the new addition as having been knocked out.
- Making your choice during the early morning quiet will aid you in staying away from that locker near the main office with the suspicious ticking sound coming from it.

General Tips

- Never pull the door closed from inside.
- Don't store ripe bananas in your locker for more than a month.

- You might as well go ahead and personalize your locker with a few pictures of friends and favorite performers, because with your allowance being what it is it would be foolish to think you could hire a decorator.

- If you have a terrible memory, you may find it convenient to scratch your combination on the back of your lock, and so you won't forget where you put it, tape a sign to your door that reads: LOOK ON THE BACK OF LOCK FOR COMBINATION.
- Don't buy locker insurance from the same senior who sold you the elevator tickets.

Sharing Lockers

- On the first day of school, find out whose father's soon being transferred to Duluth, then offer to share a locker with that student.
- Placing a plywood partition down the middle of the locker not only divides the space into equal parts, but gives you more than enough room to store a ruler, ballpoint pen refill, and all the materials you'll need to complete your wood project so long as the plans don't call for more than one dowel and a couple of strips of molding.
- If you end up sharing a locker with one of those types who takes lots of notes in class and is always checking books out of the school library, you might just as well accept the fact that when winter comes you'll have to carry your coat around with you all day.
- Boys and girls may share lockers if they agree not to peek at each other while they're changing books.

Locker Security

- The only foolproof way to avoid being robbed is by not tempting potential thieves, and the best way to accomplish this is by not locking your locker and not keeping anything it it.

There's No Place Like Home . . . Ec

In a recent nationwide survey of two high schools, it was discovered that valuable information was being omitted from the basic Home Economics course. The following, then, is a thorough and well-researched collection of timely tips and helpful hints to help turn Home Ecccccch into Home Ec. (And if this information doesn't help, this chapter is edible — so dig in!)

KITCHEN SUPPLIES: A CHECKLIST

For the Kitchen Cabinet:
  2 standard measuring cups
  1 sub-standard tin cup
  can opener
  door opener
  can closer
  potato parer
  pear parer
  partridge in a pear tree
  wire egg whip
  leather bull whip
  paring knife (5 inch)
  carving knife (9 inch)
  jack knife (¾ half-twist)
  recipe file
  nail file
  iron file (vitamin-rich recipes only)
  hot pads
  cold pads

For the Range:
  2-quart saucepan
  3-quart saucepan
  4-quart special saucepan (for re-heating
    Big Macs)
  Dutch oven
  Spanish oven
  French chef

At or Near the Sink:
  dishwasher

Optional Equipment:
  3 cotton aprons (everyday)
  2 voile and lace aprons (dress-up)
  chef's hat
  hard hat

egg poacher
animal poacher
sponge (friends excluded)

Equivalent Measures Cooks Take For Granted:
Dash — 1½ pinches
Pinch — ¼ smidge
Handful — ⅜ cup (72 pinches)
A Little — ½ handful (9 smidges)
Some — 3½ oz. (liquid measure only)
A Bunch — 2 handfuls or 6 bananas

QUICK AND EASY RECIPES:

Sugar Cookies
sugar
3 dozen cookies
Yields: 36 sugar-covered cookies

Toast
bread
toaster

Peanut Butter
1 pound shelled peanuts
hammer
Yields: a mess

Mystery Meat
restricted to school cafeteria use only

Hors d'oeuvres
bag of chips
carton french onion dip

Spaghetti
pan
can of canned spaghetti
Yields: pan of canned spaghetti

Country Steak
4 cube steaks
charcoal grill in a cow pasture
Serves: 4

Mom's Famous Apple Pie
apples
cinnamon
sugar
a famous mom

Quick Pizza
555-3000 (50¢ delivery charge)

Getting Into Trying Out

Scared of trying out? Sure, there's a lot of social pressure involved, but with our quickie tips and hints that follow, you're bound to be a shoo-in for whatever you go out for. The big clue to success is simple: don't ignore the obvious. For example. . .

You won't necessarily make the gymnastics team just because you're head over heels in love.

or

It scores no points with the judges when you throw tomatoes at your opponent on the debate team.

or

When you're going out for cheerleading, a warm and friendly smile is essential; so remember to make your smile sincere, whether you mean it or not.

and

It's probably not wise to count on a runaway victory for class treasurer just because your Uncle Harry is doing 10 to 20 in the state pen for embezzlement.

and it goes without saying that

It's not true that you have to be the tackling dummy for two weeks before you are considered for first string.

Quick Review Section

Okay, it's time for a fast review of what we've learned about school survival. Consult the chart and handy checklists below before you go on to the next section.

1. It's good behavior to accept the responsibility of calling the bus company to tell them how many seats should be reserved for the class field trip.

2. It's good behavior to ask questions while you're on a field trip to the local museum.

3. It was good behavior to whistle for the teacher when she was trying to get the students' attention on the recent field trip.

4. It's good behavior to turn your report in.

1. It's bad behavior not to include your teacher's name on the list of people needing those reserved seats.

2. It's bad behavior to choose as your first question: "Is there someplace around here where I can fill these water balloons?"

3. It was bad behavior to whistle at the teacher when she was trying to put one of her false eyelashes back on.

4. It's bad behavior to turn your report into a weapon capable of giving savage paper cuts.

5. It's good behavior to move your chair closer so you can sit at the teacher's right hand when he comes back to check on your group's research.

5. It's bad behavior to move your chair so close you're sitting *on* his right hand.

6. It's good behavior to copy what's on the board just the way the teacher wrote it.

7. It's bad behavior to copy what's on your neighbor's test paper just the way he wrote it.

8. Dropping a penny into a beaker of nitric acid to watch it fizz, bubble, and dissolve when you've got an important chemistry experiment to finish isn't exactly good behavior, but it's not all that bad either.

8. But finding a larger beaker and dropping your lab partner in it definitely is.

You Know Your Grade's Going To Be Low When . . .

1. You know your grade's going to be low when there're so many red marks on your paper you can't see the writing.

2. You know your grade's going to be low when you raise your hand and ask, "How far away from an A am I?" and the teacher says, "Do you want that in light years?"

3. You know your grade's going to be low when you offer to let the kid sitting next to you copy your answers and he turns you down.

4. You know your grade's going to be low when the teacher opens up another one of his lectures about life with: "Someday, when all of you have graduated except one . . ."

5. You know your grade's going to be low when it's the end of the school year and on book collection day the teacher says he'll collect yours *next* June.

6. You know your grade's going to be low when the teacher puts the tests in order from the highest grade down to the lowest before passing them out and by the time you get yours it's tomorrow.

7. You know your grade's going to be low when the guidance counselor keeps canceling the meeting you're supposed to have for planning next year's schedule by assuring you, "Believe me, there's no rush."

8. You know your grade's going to be low when you ask the teacher why you don't get to work problems up at the board with the rest of the class and she tells you she thought you'd get lost.

73

8 Ways To Raise A Borderline Grade Without Getting Suspended

1. Ask if you can turn in a wide-ranging but comprehensive report for extra credit, then simply staple together and turn in all the class notes you've taken since seventh grade.

2. Because all the notes you've taken since seventh grade add up to three pages, supplement your report with front and back covers, a table of contents, index, bibliography, and several pieces of shirt cardboard.

3. Offer to help your teacher when he makes up the questions for the next test.

4. If he doesn't fall for that one, try volunteering to take the test stencils down to the office to be run off.

5. Even though you don't have a car, you can score points by telling the teacher that if he ever needs a lift home he can always count on you to give him a ride on your back.

6. Greatly increase your class participation. If you think you know the answer, raise your hand, and when you don't know the answer, raise your foot.

7. Bring your teacher an apple on Monday, grapes on Tuesday, bananas on Wednesday, peaches on Thursday, and on Friday a vendor's license so she can open a fruit stand.

8. Tell your teacher you want her to know that if she's ever short on names for the A, B, or C slots and it'll help her to make the grading curve come out right, you'd be more than happy to give her permission to bump your grade up a notch, even more if she has to.

You Know You're Not Going To Get An A In Gym Class When . . .

You know you're not going to get an A in gym class when the gym teacher tells you to do 10 push-ups, and you say, "By when?"

You know you're not going to get an A in gym class when during the two-week unit on archery you talk half the class into robbing the rich and giving to the poor.

You know you're not going to get an A in gym class when you win the extra five points the teacher awards the student who is dressed first for gym — only to discover you forgot your shorts!

You know you're not going to get an A in gym class when it's your turn to lead calisthenics, and you open with 10 deep-wrist bends.

You know you're not going to get an A in gym class when the teacher tells you to climb that rope over there, and you go looking for a ladder.

You know you're not going to get an A in gym class when the quarterback on the touch football team throws a perfect spiral headed right into your hands, and you make a quick fake to the left and duck!

You know you're not going to get an A in gym class when the teacher says he's dividing the class into the red team and the gold team by lining everyone up and having each one count off, and when your turn comes, you shout, "THREE!"

You know you're not going to get an A in gym class when the gym helper starts handing out towels and announces it's time to report to the pool room, and you raise your hand to ask if your grade will be lowered because you didn't know you were supposed to bring your cue stick.

This Is A Test

The authors combed America's school waste-baskets for these test samples, and then they combed their hair before being taken to the principal's office to explain just what they thought they were doing going through the trash.

English

(The first one is done for you — after that you're on your own.)

1. **Correct any mistakes in the following sentence:**

   Us has gotta take Ralphie to the dentist next Tuesday.

   Answer: Us has gotta take Ralphie to the dentist next *Wednesday*.

2. **Locate and correct the 15 errors in the following sentence:**

   John caught the ball.

3. **Correct the punctuation in the following sentence:**

   The, dog, chased, the, cat, around, the, yard,

4. **Reading comprehension: Read the following sentence and answer the accompanying questions:**

   The lawyer for the party of the first part, being the party's partner with the Writ of Certiorari, gave the attorney for the party of the second part that part of the contractual instrument of agreement which had been instrumental in calling the plaintiff's attention to the grantor's and/or grantee's guarantee of warranted suitability when the two parties met at a party.

   This sentence means:

   a) Someone's going to lose his shirt.

   b) The one lawyer will soon by paying off his new set of golf clubs and the other one's ordered a Mercedes.

   c) If the party of the second part shows up at the party of the first part's party, he's there without an invitation.

This type of sentence is an example of
a) a compound sentence.
b) a confound sentence.
c) a suspended sentence.

5. **Reading between the lines: Read the following paragraph taken from a typical whole term endowment life insurance policy and answer the accompanying questions:**

The above paragraph means:
a) Policy owners who hold their breath until they collect on this policy are not entitled by this policy to collect.
b) Those lucky persons who own this policy are given first chance at buying scenic lots on Mars.
c) When you're ready to retire, this policy and twenty dollars will get you a cup of coffee.

6. Which of the following three choices is the correct way to diagram the sentence, "The cow jumped over the moon"?

a)

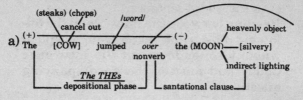

b) Nou ĭz thē tim fer ôl gud mĕn te kŭm too the ad ŭv thî kŭn' tre.

c)

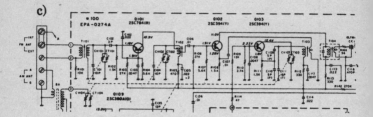

English Essays
Write a 500-word or more essay on one of the following:

1. Because so many readers have found *Silas Marner* boring, how do you suppose the author stayed awake long enough to write it?

2. Some scholars believe William Shakespeare did not write the plays and sonnets that bear his name. Compare and contrast this with your own experience of not having read any of them.

History & Government

1. **Put the following events in chronological order:**
   a) Man goes to the moon.
   b) Man discovers fire.
2. **Put the following events in chronological order:**
   a) Man bites dog.
   b) Someone invents a better mouse trap.

Multiple Guess Questions

1. World War II
   a) was second in a series.
   b) through one of those strange twists of history actually occurred before World War I.
   c) is a hard rock group whose finale includes the destruction of all its musical instruments with a small atomic bomb.
2. The Social Security Act of 1935
   a) guaranteed everyone the right to a date on Saturday night.
   b) set up the agency that issues Federal Deodorant Stamps.
   c) requires that security blankets and teddy bears be cleaned every six weeks.

True-False Questions
Put a T next to all statements that are true; put an F next to all statements that are false.

1. Those colonists who supported the American Revolution were called Whigs while those who opposed it were called Toupees.
2. Two men run together on the same ticket for President and Vice-President, then after the election they flip a coin to see who gets to be what.

3. Roosevelt's New Deal resulted in the President winning the whole pot with a pair of eights.

4. Harvest time on the American Plains was slow and arduous until Cyrus McCormick invented the grim reaper.

5. The Constitution of the United States requires that the President give his State of the Union address on television so he'll be eligible for an Emmy.

6. During the Westward expansion, American Indians were not driven from their homes, they had to walk.

Business English

1. The proper way to begin a business letter is
   a) Occupant:
   b) My Dearest Love:
   c) Now get this and get it good!

2. The proper way to close a business letter is
   a) Ciao!
   b) Gotta run!
   c) Yours 'til butter flies.
   d) And don't forget to remind me to send you a check for the postage due.

3. The proper way to close an envelope is
   a) with a stapler.
   b) with a flourish.
   c) with the letter on the inside.

4. The margins on a standard letter should
   a) not meet in the center of the page.
   b) be equal to three times the small change in your pocket.
   c) not be wide enough to drive a Mack truck through.

d) be neither here nor there, six to one and half a dozen to the other.
5. The boss calls you in and says, "Take a letter." You should say,
   a) "Where?"
   b) "I'll be happy to take a letter just as soon as I get back from taking a vacation."
   c) "Fine, which letter do you want me to take? There're 26 of them."

Shorthand

Demonstrate your mastery of Shorthand Unit 8, "Reading Other People's Mail," by matching up the notes for two important business letters from a stenographer's pad in Part I with the transcriptions in Part II.

Part I

廠大廈全部裝修完
出租不收佣金有意
八三四管理人陳洽

Letter A

陳　有　修
洽　意　完

Letter B

Part II
Letter A:
We are in receipt of your letter of the 15th and are pleased to report that your order for 6,510 phroddis handles, 8,200 torquel pins, 1,525 interimeters (unassembled), and a dozen electric finger snappers has been logged in and routed to both our Accounting and Shipping Departments. Fast service is not only our continuing goal but our future motto, thus you should receive our bill for the above items within days, and the shipment of the goods themselves will follow shortly. Please allow four to six weeks for delivery.

Letter B:
The check's in the mail.

Mathematics

Basic Review

1.

```
    98534094859209184937563229010
    21834957684300285739012748395
    10293847567483920210283746352
    48938475629376453287218237594
    36472829485069387658734625342
    37373699486746635382920938474
    33827394039299857564362998302
    76348292947854966837474753384
    15142763873484854578978974573
    77628383716615252553738389494
    73891928736554467788900289373
    77182648938492045894743637772
    92875843989740598695363552637
    13579097653432145788654326796
    12787654382987675890876565754
    12768387879082786367263526398
    18927394857001237788372930293
    12867382974649583729302037463
  +48293827384930293847483847 3883
```

2. Round off to the nearest hundreth: 100
3. What number is missing from the following series?

   $2, 9, 16, 53, 97, 276, 359, 4, 250, \underline{\ ?\ }, 11, 71, 86$

4. 89
    93
   −42

Algebra

1.

   A
   X
   Y
   N
  +Z

2.

   Y
  −X

3. Solve for Q:

$$\frac{6X-5Y+MY=9-4ZX\ (WK-RP)\,12-6(BVD)\,[4]^2}{2B-(10A+10B)-rxt[TV-NBC]+54-40X}$$

Math Thought Problems

1. If a man on a 125-ft. tower drops a 12-lb. iron ball and a 3-lb. block of pine at the same time and there is a man 5′ 12″ tall standing directly beneath and 47-ft. below the falling block of wood, how far in both metric and ASA units will the man on the ground be able to travel before his car's 10-gallon gas tank will need to be refilled?

2. A man buys 2 lbs. of 6-penny nails, two 55-lb. bags of grass seed, and a half dozen 100-watt light bulbs at the hardware store, then a pound and a half of peaches, 2 lbs. of salted peanuts, a large loaf of sandwich rye, and three green peppers on special for 79¢ at the supermarket. How many days remain until the man gets his next pay check?

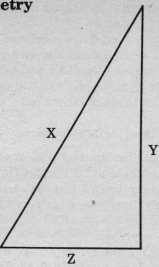

Figure XYZ is a
   a) right triangle.
   b) left triangle.
   c) Bermuda Triangle.
   d) scarf.

General Science
True-False Questions

Put a T next to all statements that are true; put an F next to all statements that are false.

1. The planet Pluto was named after the ancient Greek God of Cartoon Characters.
2. Galileo made one of man's great scientific breakthroughs when he peered into his telescope and discovered that the girl who lived three streets away preferred red hair ribbons.
3. Because the United States is a democratic country, when American scientists split the

atom, they split it into equal parts so every citizen gets his share.
4. If a quarter is placed in a beaker of sulfuric acid it will become small and worthless in a matter of minutes, but this will be a great deal slower than the effect on the same coin of the current rate of inflation.

Science Essay Questions

1. If it is true that gravity and atmospheric pressure combine to keep water from being raised higher than 32 feet above sea level, why do they have those little paper drinking cups in airplane lavatories?
2. Using the formula $E = MC^2 - 3.14$, how many foot candles of work does it take to move a one-hundred-pound weight up a 42° incline if it just doesn't want to go?
3. How much wood would a woodchuck chuck if a woodchuck could chuck wood?
4. Why is it inappropriate to say that a woodchuck who has increased the amount of wood chucked has upchucked?

Biology

Understanding Our Green Plants
1. What happens if a green plant is deprived of water for more than a year?
2. What happens to a green plant if it is placed in the oven at 350° for 40 minutes?
3. How often should a green plant see its dentist?
4. At what age should you tell a green plant it's adopted? How old should the plant be?

Dissecting Mr. Specimen

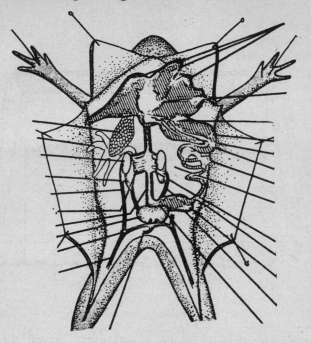

1. The drawing above illustrates
   a) the convenience of the new easy-opening frog.
   b) the quickest route to the sophomore class picnic.
   c) how to carve your Thanksgiving turkey.
   d) how to change the plugs in a '77 Ford.

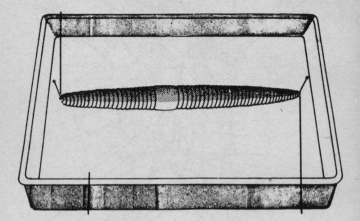

2. The picture above illustrates Cagwell's Third Law of Biology, which is:

a) Let sleeping worms lie.

b) Specimens supplied by American Worm and Frog come neatly packed in roomy containers you can later use to store leftovers.

c) The smart shopper can save up to 40% when ordering french fries and cole slow as part of the Worm-in-a-Basket budget meal.

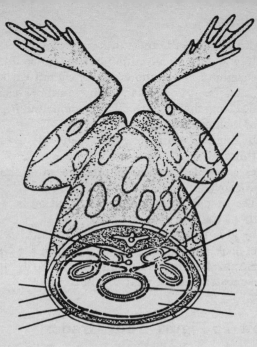

3. The specimen pictured above is
   a) a ham with flippers.
   b) the famous storybook character, the Headless Frogman.
   c) a type of frog with an exceptionally low I.Q.
   d) a good example of "power dissecting" using the wood shop's circular saw.

Chemistry

Multiple Guess Questions

1. If you mix dicalcium phosphate, sodium caseinate, manganous oxide, colbalt carbonate, choline chloride, and aminobenzoic acid together, the resulting compound is
   a) banana creme pie.
   b) harmful only to granite and all living things.
   c) ordered as a pizza topping less often than anchovies.

2. The best way to balance an equation is
   a) at the end of the month.
   b) give it to your father's accountant.
   c) look around for the kid who won the National Science Foundation Award last semester and sit next to him.

How To Figure Your Grade:

Step One

Questions are each worth 22 points. After allowing for a margin of error, each answer is worth 20. The only exceptions are as follows:

For every item answered
incorrectly, give yourself .... 25 points

For every item with an illegible
answer, give yourself .... 12 points

For every item you drew a complete
blank on, give yourself .... 5 points

For every item that already had a
complete blank drawn on it at
the printer's, give yourself .... 5 points

For remembering to put your name
on your paper, give yourself ..... 10 points

For having enough sense to put
  someone else's name on your
  paper, give yourself .... 20 points
For throwing this test in the
  wastebasket after reading the
  first question, give yourself ..... 250 points

Step Two

Add up the total accumulated points in each
column. Multiply the sum by 2, then divide that
answer in half. The resulting score is called the
Standardized Classroom Objective Ritten
Evaluation (SCORE).

Congratulations!
You are
now a
BANANAS
student!

The Last Word

Just because you read most of *The BANANAS B- Guide To School Survival* to yourself without moving your lips doesn't mean the book's not full of sound advice. The changes you've already noticed at school prove this.

No longer do your teachers stand out from everyone else on the faculty because of the extra red markers they had to carry just so they wouldn't run out of ink grading your papers. Two of the school's guidance counselors are arguing over who should have the movie rights to your case history.

Don't you think you've earned a little time off? Of course you do. So just fill in these official-looking official forms, keeping in mind they'll probably look a bit more realistic if you remove them from the book before handing them to some unsuspecting teacher. Quicker than you can say, "Can't you take a joke!?" the forms will have gotten you out of class, out of school, and if you're not careful, into trouble!

OFFICIAL REQUEST-FOR-PUPIL REQUEST FORM

Please send _____
(Name of Pupil Who's Going to be Sent)

[   ] immediately
[   ] if not sooner
[   ] if he ever shows up
[   ] if and when
[   ] by next Tuesday

from Room # _____, along with an OFFICIAL HALL PASS FORM, to:

[   ] take a powder
[   ] talk a walk
[   ] take a picture
[   ] take a bus
[   ] take off
[   ] take a bath
[   ] take one
[   ] take two, they're small
[   ] take a vacation
[   ] the hamburger stand up the street
[   ] the pizza parlor down the street
[   ] the blue Ford in the fourth row of the student parking lot
[   ] the [   ] boy or [   ] girl of his/her dreams

_____
(Official-looking Signature)

OFFICIAL HALL PASS FORM

Note: The individual herein named on this Official Hall Pass Form is entitled to and has the full privileges and permissibles that go with and are a part of the Official Hall Pass Form when signed, sealed, but not necessarily delivered by a school principal, school mascot, or school bus, and should under few circumstances be stopped, detained, bothered, harassed, bugged or tweeked by hall guards, prison guards, bank guards, fender guards, Right Guard, left guards, left tackles, teachers on duty, cabbies off duty, truant officers, law officers, officers of the day, or PTA Room Mothers.

_____ has permission as out-
(Name Student Is Using)
lined above to be near, in, and around the halls as follows:

Date: _____

Period: _____

Day of Week: _____

Purpose: _____

_____
(Signature, Mark, or Rubber Stamp of Dismissing Person)